Made for Each Other

WILLIAM STEIG

JOANNA COTLER BOOKS

An Imprint of HarperCollinsPublishers

Made for Each Other

Copyright © 2000 by William Steig

Printed in the U.S.A. All rights reserved.

http://www.harpercollins.com

Library of Congress Cataloging-in-Publication Data

Steig, William, 1907–

    Made for each other / William Steig.

        p.   cm.

    "Joanna Cotler books."

    Summary: Devoted couples declare their love and explain what they mean to each other.

    ISBN 0-06-028512-5. — ISBN 0-06-028513-3 (lib. bdg.)

    [1. Love—Fiction.]   I. Title.

PZ7.S8177Mad   2000   99-26425

[E]—dc21   CIP

Typography by Alicia Mikles

1 2 3 4 5 6 7 8 9 10

❖

First Edition

To Jeanne, of course

I love the hay you walk on.

You make this blossom blush.

You slay me.

We dance to the same music.

I'd kill for you.

You keep me on my toes.

You be the beauty, I'll be the beast.

Our love is magical.

We were made for each other.

You're just ducky.

You're the cat's meow.

 In spite of everything, I love you.

It's bound to work out.

We're always in step.

Where there's smoke, there's fire.

But you *know* you love me.

There's nothing I wouldn't do for you.

Our love is eternal.

We remain true to our vows.

We sometimes have those foolish little spats.

The road is often bumpy.

Till death do us part.